SEASON ENDING

6 Stages of Athletic Transition

BY
R.J. SUMRALL

DEDICATION

I dedicate this book first to my wife and children. Second, to all those that raised, mentored, coached, and advised me throughout my journey.

I ask, how do I start a book that will connect with my readers in a powerful way—

The answer is—*I Pray.*

Father God, I pray over the readers of this book. I pray you open their minds to the information on these pages. Bless them with great understanding and the ability to turn this found knowledge into wisdom so they have immeasurable success navigating the stages of athletic transition—

in Jesus's mighty name.

Amen.

Contents

INTRODUCTION

You enter and see the bright lights, hear the cheers, and loud music. The energy is indescribable. You eventually feel the beads of sweat—the labored breathing makes you feel alive. The smell of the locker room... good or bad, it is a fond and fleeting memory. There is nothing quite like it. The rush of adrenaline gives you a heightened awareness. You are like a superhero—super speed, superhuman strength. With every noise and slight twitch of the competition, we are like a predator on prey. The timing of the pounce is choreographed in milliseconds.

When you are a high performing athlete, you capture the attention of the spectators, fans, family, friends—and if lucky enough, you make it to the big leagues where everything is amplified times ten.

High performing athletes train for hours a day—day in and day out. The vision and focus are intense because the competition is equally intense. Athletes breathe, live, and sleep in the sports structure of fine tuning every detail.

But what happens when the music stops... and the lights dim? The daily ritual gone. The cheers were gone, replaced by the deafening silence. If you are a former athlete, you may know the answer.

The adrenaline disappears and in its place is an unrecognizable emptiness—an itch that you can no longer scratch. A shadow feeling that you cannot describe. The physical need for the rush is like withdrawal—sometimes unbearable. We live in a society where we are what we do. So, if we spent every hour of every day on being an athlete, what are you when you are no longer in the game?

There is a sense of loss—loss of purpose, focus—loss of identity. How do you transition from athlete to former athlete when that is all you know, and it was all you were?

The answers do not come easy. Identity crisis is a genuine crisis and one that former athletes struggle with. I know. I had a dream that consumed me.

This aspiration would distract me from my schoolwork and got me into trouble during class. My dream woke me and fueled me to work hard. It gave me the grit to grind through the most challenging moments. My vision allowed me to detach from reality and see the Promised Land. But just like Moses, my dream got cut short.

When I was a young boy, my dream was to play in the NFL—what a dream!

At five, I earned the nickname Parkay, after Parkay butter. My older cousins named me that because I was as smooth as butter on the field. No, it wasn't because I had butterfingers.

Some say being good at a sport takes passion and talent, while others will argue it is effort. Back then, I didn't know or follow everything about football. To be honest, I write this as a thirty-six-year-old father of four and still don't follow everything football—funny thing is, I prefer to watch track meets over football games. For me, I was good at football, but I put in the effort and rose through the ranks.

Eventually, the music and cheers stopped, and I had to figure out how to transition from being an athlete to living as a former athlete. It was a time of uncertainty, frustration, anger, and depression. This war with self is an identity crisis and common among high performing athletes who are trying to transition into main society. So, you are not alone.

I see you—I was you.

I wrote this book because I fought my battles alone. I had to figure out how to transition from being an athlete to living as a former athlete. What I can tell you is you will be at war with yourself. The battle you fight is the identity crisis you did not expect. You fight through stages of anger and depression while seeking glory and purpose again.

The problem is we do not give athletes the tools to fight this battle. I did not have the guidance and had to fight my way through the stages of transition through trial by fire. You do not have to take that path. Between these pages, you will find the tools to fight your battle. I will guide you through the stages of anger, avoidance, depression, glory chasing, calling—and finally appreciation. Unlike me, you do not have to go to battle alone.

Between the covers, you will get a glimpse of my stories— struggles and triumphs—so you know I come from a place of genuine understanding. You will learn the stages of athletic transition you go through and how to conquer them.

Along the way, I offer inspiration through my deep-seated faith, but will not preach at you. I humbly serve and therefore pass no judgment. The reference to religious passages is for their beauty and relevance to what you may go through. If you rock with Christianity or not, I honestly feel the words will move you. There is an assumption that our stories are similar, and my perspective comes from coaching and not therapy.

Full disclosure: I am not a therapist or a doctor. So, if you feel you need more than coaching, more than comradery—if you feel you are in a much darker place—please seek the advice of a qualified medical professional.

CHAPTER 1

MY BEGINNING

"Every new beginning comes from some other beginning's end."
~ Seneca

You are embarking on a journey by starting on the rough side of the mountain. If you thought chasing your dream was hard, I encourage you never to leave your dream without putting on your armor. This is a trek that many have ventured on, and most never reach the top.

I will assume, like me, your dream of having an illustrious career in your respective sport fueled every action. You connected the choices you made in and outside your sport to achieving the ultimate dream. My dream was to go to the National Football League. Yours may have been to be a professional Olympic athlete. No matter the sport, there was total commitment to the wondrous vision ahead. We even acted upon some of our poor decisions because of our dreams. I know I did.

In eighth grade, I understood that if you look good; you play good. I did not understand the connection at the time, but studies in social science reveal that our physical appearance plays an important role in our experiences and opportunities. When we like the way we look, it boosts our confidence. Confidence is king. So, even those athletes that look less put together can be dawgs out there in their sport. Nevertheless, when you *think* you look good, you feel good, which allows you to be free and play with creativity to maximize your talents.

Now, it is important to rewind the tape and look at that replay. "When you think you look good, you feel good, which allows you to be free and play with creativity to maximize your talents." Drop that wisdom nugget into your safe because that is a life tool.

To look good, I made a terrible choice (or choices) that directly impacted my dream. In eighth grade, my best friend and I went shopping at Sports Authority. This store was an athlete's heaven on earth. It had any and everything athletes needed to look good for maximizing one's talents. We were two young males with a dream and a wallet full of air. Yep—you guessed it. Our fingers became really sticky. I don't recall either of us coming up with a plan, but we both left with items. The thrill was like scoring a touchdown or making a new personal record.

Between August to October fifteenth, my buddy and I went to Sports Authority to frequently shop using our five-finger discount. We stole gloves, wristbands, mouthpieces, socks—pretty much anything we could fit in our pants or mouths. Little did we know the store had a beat on us.

I should have known and stopped while we were ahead.

I believe God gives us warning signs, and I got mine. First, I got caught stealing a bike from another apartment complex—I talked my way out. I ignored the sign. Then, I almost got caught with a different friend at a Kmart trying to steal walkie-talkies. You know that voice in your head or the little guys that sit on your shoulders—one good, one bad. Maybe it is that gut feeling. Well, call it what you will, but the Holy Spirit told me to leave them.

Thank God I listened because, on my way out, the loss prevention person stopped us. We were empty-handed and went home Scot-free. What do they say, "a hard head makes a soft behind"—lol.

One day, my buddy and I were planning to go on our weekly shopping tour, but this day was different. My older cousin, by one grade, had teammates over. They knew what we were about to do and gave us a grocery list of items they wanted us to get. We happily obliged. My cousin, who knew what we were doing the entire time, told me not to go, but I was like, I'm good; I will be right back. Well, I didn't come back.

As we were walking out of the store, a man with tethered gray bum-looking sweatpants stood in front of us as we exited the store and asked, "where's my merchandise?"

After the second time asking that question, I realized he was a cop. Yes, as you can imagine, they awarded me with some steel bracelets that absolutely did not look good.

Now, you might think that was the lowest of the lows in my life, but it wasn't.

I believe God makes a way out of no way. You see, the next day was my mother's birthday. What a terrible present—it sucked. I got the opportunity to ride in the back of the police car. I modeled the jumpsuit for the Orange County juvenile detention center. They thought so highly of me they took my one-of-a-kind autograph, my fingerprints. They even gave me my own room, which had a bed made of concrete, no pillow or blanket, and glass windows and doors so I could see all the other kids sitting in chairs watching TV.

My stepdad made me stay there overnight, letting me imagine my mother's torment. Breaking her heart was the worst part of it all.

So, where is God in this story?

There were only a few people who caught wind of my situational sleepover. On Sunday, we went to church. It was your typical Black church, and if you have no clue what a Black church is like, no book or video will give it justice, so you should visit one. After church, I'm walking to the car with my head down, and tail tucked. My mother and little brother were both on my left. My pastor, Pastor Brown, stopped me in my tracks. And to my knowledge, he had no clue that I was arrested for shoplifting two days prior. As a twelve-year-old boy, I received some heaven-in-earth-shaking news.

God makes himself known in hell. As a twelve-year-old, my situation felt as close to hell as one my age could get. You might say, things happen for a reason. Whichever the case, Pastor

Brown calls after me, "RJ, I had a vision from God I must share with you."

I say nothing, but I'm thinking, *let's go! I'm going to be an NFL superstar*.

Well, Pastor Brown's words were so out of left field, no one could believe it. "RJ, the vision I had from God is that you are going to be a pastor."

My brain screamed, *WHAT! NOPE*.

Sure, I went to church, but wasn't a Christian and I didn't understand the importance of Jesus. Of course, I prayed to God, but Jesus was just some dude that died. Being a Christian was not something I wanted to be. Let's just say that the attitudes and behaviors of particular people in church were less than motivational. I judge God's Kingdom by the citizens rather than the king.

That one sentence is worth the tape rewind and replay, "I judge God's Kingdom by the citizens rather than the king."

I became a Christian many years later but didn't forget Pastor Brown's vision. Many times, our purpose or path is revealed to us. Maybe God has revealed something to you, but you could be like me—you rejected it or were oblivious to it. After my encounter with Pastor Brown, I decided to make better choices after my run-in with the law. My choices became laser focused on my sport and dream. It was less than a direct path and I had to scratch and fight for position. In the end, the inevitable happens to us all and we have to transition from current athlete to former athlete and this transition is one of the hardest battles you will fight.

COACHING SESSION

Take some time to answer the questions below:

- How does becoming a former athlete effect how you see yourself?

- What things in your past have had a significant impact on making you who you are today?

- What words have been spoken to you that gave you a glimpse of who you are to be after the game is over?

CHAPTER 2

AVOIDANCE

*"Emotions are continually affecting our thought processes
and decisions, below the level of our awareness. And the most
common emotion of them all is the desire for pleasure and the
avoidance of pain."*
~ Robert Greene

The first four stages of your athletic transition are not in a systematic order. Like the stages of grief, you may experience them randomly. Each stage could last longer than others. Your journey will be unique, but I can tell you this: If your sense of identity intertwines with being an athlete, you will experience all four stages before you find your calling.

I start with avoidance even though it could come after anger or simultaneously. Avoidance is our natural answer to our fight, flight, or freeze response. Sometimes, the battle that rages within is too great and we feel our only option is to flee or freeze. Avoidance is the flee or freeze. We refuse to move forward or we run from reality and do not deal with it.

Being an athlete, we look for triggers. We look for competitive advantages, and as I read the definition of avoidance, the word *shun* jumps out from the page. To shun something is to keep away from a place, person, or object—from motives of dislike, caution; you take pains to avoid. For example, when a relationship is over, both individuals do not want to fight, so they avoid each other in a graceful dance of fleeing, and they are frozen from moving on due to fear. What we know is better than the unknown. Humans dislike change. At first, they avoid each other because the other is the trigger. Eventually, one or both conclude they need to travel away from each other's path to move on. They can no longer avoid the trigger.

Avoiding the trigger will only make things worse. You begin to have a toxic relationship with yourself.

~❖~

After the NFL draft, I had a smile on my face. I still had dollars and a dream and was confident I would get a call to be a free agent. I waited day after day after day—and nothing. One of my best friends received a call and got his shot. From there, I knew that if they gave me a shot, I would make the team.

I waited some more.

My best friend would try to encourage me by saying I should be in the NFL. He would tell me I was better than some wide receivers currently playing. But as I sat on my girlfriend's couch, I knew I had to do something because my NFL dreams were ending. So, one day I got up and found a job.

I told everyone—my first job out of college was being a bouncer at a bar.

Being a bouncer—what a perfect job for someone who wants to hit people for a living. I enjoyed myself, but my journey of avoidance began. People would notice me and immediately talk about what an excellent athlete I was. They were star struck. In their jubilation, they would ask, "why didn't you go to the NFL? You were a stud."

I would give the heads up shoulder shrug, indicating I didn't know with a smile. I no longer wanted to be known as the football player or athlete. It was too painful. I avoided the athlete within me by pushing him into a box. No one knew my pain, and no one thought to ask me why I avoided it. They saw me as a college athlete, and they see you as a special person who went to the top because you were a college or supreme athlete. Why? Because only a few get to play after high school.

People asked me to play on their flag football team, but as much as my athlete wanted to come out, I would say no because of the pain. He would be let out occasionally, but only for sports that had no future for me. I played sand volleyball, frisbee golf, golf, and ultra-marathons. Marathons were long distance obstacle courses, but football was my trigger and not permitted.

The other way of avoiding my trigger was to never watch football on TV. Between graduating at twenty-two until my early thirties, it was painful. Watching the NFL was the worst because all I did was compare myself to those living my dream.

I would see guys I played against that I knew I outperformed—doing what I thought I was called for. People would talk to me about players I played with or against in high school or college, and they would be over the moon excited, but their enthusiasm buried me. They were supposed to be talking about me and my game.

I eventually went back to my alma mater because my wife's family were huge Iowa State football fans. If it weren't for my wife, I would have never gone back. After graduation, I avoided college football in my heart for about four to six years. I took part, but I was walking with my eyes closed. I hated going to the actual games; sitting with fans is hard because they think they know the game, but they have no clue, and all you want to do is shut them up. While sitting there, I would think, *I shouldn't be here, I should be playing in the NFL. I should be living out my dream, not sitting with you listening to you talk about what you would do if you were down there.*

Tailgating was my only sense of joy. Other than that, I didn't go all in for my alma mater. I blocked them out of my heart and focused on running away from college football and especially my alma mater because of the pain. The game was irrelevant, but tailgating became my escape.

If, like me, they trained us to never let them see you sweat. Never show fear—push through the pain by ignoring it. Because of this, you might not even know you are avoiding your past. So, my story is to shine a spotlight on your avoidance. When you realize you have been avoiding the past—the triggers—you might turn angry, frustrated, or even sad. It's okay to feel this way; it is part of the healing process.

For me, Jesus is the comforter and I ask you to release your pain upon Him. He knows what to do with it. He knows how to heal a broken heart. When you recognize your avoidance, seek to know the pain. If you do not, you could end up like many other athletes. I have seen many teammates and opponents fall into the trap of drugs, alcohol, sex, and pornography. These things are worthless healers. They are like band-aids to a broken leg.

One such friend was a phenomenal baseball player and hurt his back. His baseball career was over. To heal his pain, he prescribed himself alcohol as a healing agent. As he spiraled down through avoidance of the sport, he had an encounter with the Lord. My buddy was desperate and considering the darkest option with a gun in hand to end his suffering when he asked God to save him. His prayers were answered, and he worked hard to make his way back on top. He is doing well and reaching for new dreams.

You will hear me say this many times: name the pain and give it to Jesus. However, I know how lost you can feel. Sometimes, you know the pain is there but cannot define it. It is a shadow feeling. We can also have difficulty in finding Jesus. We question whether He can hear us in times of difficulty. For these reasons, you often need support.

Find a person who has gone through your journey and made it to the top of the mountain. If you don't have that person, find a trusted Christian leader and open up. And if you don't have that, reach out to a former teammate and read through this book together. Then set up times to discuss what you have read.

God will provide the person or group if you ask Him. Know that it is okay to feel lost or uncertain, but it's not okay to bury your feelings. To move on means to let it go.

~❖~

It took me a while to learn to hand over my pain and work to let go. I worked as a bouncer for five or so months but needed to make more money. So, I started to scout other options. Helzberg Diamonds interviewed me, and they hired me as an assistant manager. I liked my job and was on the path to becoming a store manager. One day, this young man came in and wanted help with finding the right diamond ring for his future fiancé. After talking for a while and showing him pieces, he asked me my name. I told him RJ Sumrall. His eyes grew twice the size. It was like he had seen a movie star.

He immediately asked, "Why are you here? Why aren't you in the NFL?"

He asked like it was my choice to work in retail and forgo my dream. I thought I was getting over it, but all I did was suppress the hurt and avoided the feeling of not accomplishing my dream. I was fooling myself. The reminders would always pop up, just like they did with this young man. The question was always "why"—

It was the beginning of realizing that I knew I was created for more.

I shared this story to tell you if you don't name the pain, allow it to work through you, and give it away, it will fester and later reveal itself like an open wound. God created you for more—never settle. Dream big and chase it. Just because your childhood dreams didn't happen doesn't mean you are supposed to stop dreaming and chasing. God created you to do amazing things for his Kingdom through a unique calling. It's your job to find it.

Don't worry; I got you, and I'm going to help you find your calling. Finding your purpose is a journey and you have to work through the stages of transition to get there. I am here to guide you. It begins with recognizing and working through the avoidance. You cannot suppress the reality that you need to confront. Avoidance is a barrier to discovering the grand design—the calling—God has for you. If you do not work through the avoidance, you create a barrier to the grand design God has for you.

Rewind the tape and replay: If you do not work through the avoidance, you create a barrier to the grand design God has for you.

For inspiration, read the first chronicles 11:22-25. It is a story from thousands of years ago. A young man named Benaiah was made to do great things for God's Kingdom. One day he chased a lion into a pit on a snowy day. Because of his bravery, Benaiah became the general of God's military "Israel." Like Benaiah, you were made to fight lions and do great things.

COACHING SESSIONS

Read Chronicles 11:22-25

- What did you feel reading that story?
- How does that story apply to you today?
- Where is your lion of opportunity?
- Are you willing to chase the lion?
- If you see yourself avoiding, what are some things to ease yourself back in?
- How can you keep avoidance from making you complacent to chase future opportunities?
- Create a list of people you can invite to go on this journey of transition with you.

CHAPTER 3

ANGER

"Anger is an acid that can do more harm to the vessel in which it is stored than to anything on which it is poured."
~ Mark Twain

Anger often comes in waves. Sometimes our triggers and anger are like the moon's effect on the tide. Predictable. We know when it will rear its ugly head. But, other times, it comes like a bolt of lightning. Unexpected and out of nowhere.

I share my story when the guy alluded to me choosing to not pursue the NFL and work in retail selling jewelry. Talk about boiling anger. The tide comes in and now I wasn't angry with him, but I was angry with everybody that had a stake in my future—my dream.

The anger brought memories to the surface.

When I was a high school senior, I dreamed of going to the University of Miami to play football. They were recruiting me, and it seemed like my dream would come true. When I was in high school, Miami was the team to beat, ranking number one or number two in the nation and in my backyard. My hometown is Orlando, Florida.

My desire to go there wasn't a pipe dream. Then, it was more real than I could have ever imagined, but I didn't know it at the time. I was a highly recruited wide receiver and free safety coming out of Florida. I ranked in the top ten of my class in both positions and seen as one of the top track athletes heading into my senior year. You could say I had a golden ticket to my dreams. Well, unless someone else has the ticket in their hand.

Many times, I would hear from scouts about not receiving tapes from my head coach, per their request. You see, my head coach, unbeknownst to me, was not one to help with the recruiting process. He was a user, not a promoter. My coach tried his best to stall my advancement, but the Lord God had his hand on me. I had to take it upon myself to promote and petition myself.

My plan was getting myself into a conference All-Star game, but it was extremely hard work. The Florida-Georgia All-Star game I pursued vehemently said no. I couldn't get them everything they needed to decide whether they wanted me to be on the team because of the lack of cooperation from my high school head coach.

My efforts eventually paid off as I got into a lower level All-Star game. Going into practice and into the game, I used it for all it was worth. Little did I know God was watching over his plan. There was a coach from Iowa State University scouting another kid who saw me at practice. It didn't take long for him to notice me and take an interest in recruiting me.

At some point, the linebackers coach of my team came up to me and said, "I'm going to help you get to college." I believe he knew what was happening behind the scenes and felt sorry for me.

Of course, my signing day was one for the books. In high school, there was one signing day, the first week of February. I met the beginning of that day with sadness, but before track practice began, it ended with a celebration. On national signing day, one school offered me a scholarship. Of course, with my stats and talent, I thought I would have gotten more, but something was better than nothing.

Within the last hour of signing day, the Iowa State football coaches called my linebackers coach instead of my head coach and offered me a scholarship to continue my football dream. The scholarship they offered me was their last and final scholarship.

I stated God was working on His plan because when my mother met me at home, she said I was going to Iowa State because God had a plan for my life. I looked her in her eyes and said I was going to Iowa State because God knows my plan, and he's working on my plan. Little did I know my mother was right.

Back then, I had no idea that my head coach had told every school that offered me a scholarship through him to not proceed with offering me an opportunity to play for their school. The coach even told South Florida that I had already graduated.

I had only later learned of my coach's activities behind my back. While training for the NFL, I ran into a coach who worked for the University of Miami football team. After a day's worth of training, he came up to me, "RJ Sumrall—I remember you from my days at the University of Miami. You went to Winter Park High School. We offered you a scholarship, and your head coach told us not to offer it to you, so we rescinded the offer."

Now, some might think I had a reputation or was a terrible dude. The high school coach knew something others didn't. That is not the case. After eighth grade, I had no trouble with the law. I had a 3.2 GPA and was friends with all the administration and students. Even the coach's grandkids were friends. Raised by parents of deep Southern heritage, I also respected my elders.

Still, to this day, I do not know my coach's reasoning, but I know I wasn't the only one. Supposedly, he tried to sabotage my older cousin's career too, but he was the eleventh-ranked quarterback in the nation, so our head coach could not sabotage his journey. Since then, the school inducted me into my high school's Hall of Fame for football and track. So, you can say I probably deserved the opportunity to pursue my dream of playing football at the highest level.

I share this story to help you understand some of my brewing anger. I say brewing because my struggles were not over. My high school coach wasn't the only person I was angry with. I was angry with my former college head coach, too.

After our last game, I had my final meeting with my college coach. He encouraged me, but our relationship was a little tricky. During his first year as a head coach, I won the number one starting wide receiver position as a junior. Everyone knew the

Z position would be our quarterback's primary target based on the design of the offense, and I was that guy.

This was significant because the year before, under the previous coach, I had to wait my turn, and I was the third starting receiver on the depth chart. The previous number-one receiver decided not to pursue the NFL as a junior. He had two great performing seasons in one of the toughest conferences in college football. He was known as one of the top receivers in college football, and I tried my best to encourage him to leave early so I could start as the number one receiver and he could become a millionaire. But he stayed for his senior season with a new head coach. So, you can say I beat him for the number one spot—my future was looking bright.

Early in the season, my NFL pursuit got a ding. Tuesday was our intense day. I was doing a blocking drill against a running back who was working with the scout team. He was 5'5", and ran a 4.4-4.5, 40-yard dash, so he was fast and explosive and could squat 500 pounds. I squatted 450 pounds. At the start of the drill, I was standing in a receiver stance, and to accomplish a good block, you have to get in an excellent athletic squatting position for explosion. My buddy was only a foot or two away from me at the start of the drill, so my receivers coach said hike, and this 5'5" running back drove me backward for five yards. While he is demolishing me in this drill, I'm laughing because I know that this would never happen in real football. They knew me as one of the best-blocking receivers on our team and I took pride in my job.

Well, displeased with the results of the blocking drill, the strength conditioning coach marched to the head coach and snitched on me. The head coach comes over and starts ripping me a new one. During my tongue lashing, I'm trying to get my chin strap over my lips because I'm a habitual smiler. It's my defense mechanism when I get in trouble. I knew it was happening because I had had many unfriendly situations with my mother before this incident. I didn't think it was funny, but nonverbal communication is 58% of communication. So, the coach barks his inquisition, "are you f'ing smiling?!"

I began to say I was sorry, but that didn't cool his jets.

The next thing out of his mouth rocked my world. "You won't be seeing the field; you're benched!"

He demoted me from the starting first receiver to the eleventh receiver on the depth chart. It took me three weeks to become a starter again, but I was no longer the first target; I was the second target sitting in the X position. This move made it harder for me to get my first touchdown, which I did not accomplish until my senior year.

My senior year was a good year. I racked up some great statistics, but my team sucked. We went five and nineteen under the new head coach in my junior and senior years. Though we sucked as a team, I would always wonder how my life would have been different if that blocking drill had never happened. Maybe I would have accomplished my dream.

After the season, I sat down with my coach. He told me, "RJ, you are a wonderful man, and I know you want to go to the NFL. You are an NFL caliber player."

Now I believe in what he was saying because, as you know, coaches shoot the information straight and they do not shy away from painful details. So, when a coach gives you adoration, you know it's real. I also believed my coach's words because of the caliber of players he coached throughout his coaching career and all the NFL players he has had experience with. He told me he would push to get me into the NFL. That was all I needed to hear.

Through my NFL pursuit, I learned your coach is a huge proponent of getting a shot in the Indianapolis combine and NFL. I felt my coach had my back. Well, a few weeks later, he left my school to coach at the University of Auburn, and in his transition, he brushed all the Iowa State dust off his shoes. That included me—same story, different coach, different day.

They did not invite me to the Indianapolis combine, and I missed the spot by twelve people. Again, it felt like high school, where I was fighting to be included in All-Star games.

I didn't have time to dwell on not being invited to the combine. Rather, I jumped into my training in Florida and put all my eggs in my school's Pro Day. This is where NFL scouts come to look at your attributes and skills. During the Pro Day, I had some impeccable statistics.

I jumped a vertical of thirty-nine inches and benched 225 pounds seventeen times. My 40-yard dash took 4.4 seconds. Coming in at just under six-foot-one and weighing 215 pounds, I ran my routes smoothly and caught everything thrown at me. I performed like a professional. My reputation was for smooth and precise routes in sure hands and someone who could play all receiver positions plus kickoff returner and punt returner. So, at worse, I knew I was going to get a shot.

When the time came for the NFL draft, I was told that I might get picked up in the fourth round by Buffalo from my agent. Then I was told in the fifth and sixth rounds that the Jacksonville Jaguars would pick me up. And then, in the final round, I was told I was going to be picked up as Mr. irrelevant by the Kansas City Chiefs. The Chiefs picked a punter as Mr. Irrelevant. The news didn't discourage me because I knew someone would pick me up as a free agent, and I just had to wait a few days and get the phone call.

I got nothing.

And I blamed it on my coach—for all that happened—from the benching to his leaving. Every year for about eight years, I would be reminded of my anger, knowing people who didn't grade out or put up football numbers like me got a shot at their dream.

While working my retail job, I had no clue the anger was just under the surface. It wasn't until that conversation with the young man that I awakened to the facts. The fact was I was mad at everybody, even my girlfriend, who had nothing to do with my dream. I even directed my anger at God. God received the bulk of my anger.

I believed he created me to be a football player; he created me to be a super athlete. My thought was my plans were his plan because he continued to bless my journey. But the journey I was on—the journey you are on—is to get us closer to your purpose. You can do so through your faith.

I know because back then, I knew of God, went to church and attended Chapel and Bible studies. But remember this: God does his best work when we are weak and stuck in the trenches. The week I got benched for the first time, and the only time of my life, I received Jesus as my savior that Friday in Lincoln, Nebraska. My Christian birthday is on October 5th, 2007.

I later opened my eyes to see that God had a different plan that he would reveal. God has a plan for your life, too. I pray God will open your heart, your mind, and your eyes so you will see what he designed you for, like he did for me.

Right now, you are angry. I know you're angry, and it's okay to be mad. Never think or let someone tell you, you should not be upset. You have worked so hard for so many years chasing a future, and it's over for whatever reason. Yes, be mad, but you have to move through it. Give it to God through Jesus. Jesus tells us to take up his yoke, for it is easy and gives us rest—peace. Matthew 11: 28-30.

I warn you to be careful with your anger and, most importantly, be careful who you direct your anger toward. Don't forget, He is the creator, and you are the creation. He's all powerful, all knowing, all loving, all grace filled, in all mercy. Bring your pain to Him, but with respect. He is a king! You do not want Him to turn His back and allow you to control your life. He did with me, and I almost ruined my life because of my pain and frustration.

Remember this phrase: Hurt people, hurt people. Don't stay in hell if you don't have to. Your anger will grow into bitterness, and bitterness destroys the beholder in all things and those around them; you must get away and take a new yoke. Don't allow this pain and anger to devour or direct you because it will cause you to crash and lose everything. Your soul is more important than your dream. Anger rots out the vessel—you are the vessel.

Rewind the tape and play back: Anger rots out the vessel—you are the vessel.

When you wake and find that you have been avoiding the process, and eventually feel the anger you kept down for so long, you often become depressed. You may flow in and out of the stages of transition from anger and depression and back to avoidance. It is not a shot to the goal posts—it is a process. Remember, you must keep moving.

COACHING SESSION

- What are some things you can do that bring you pure joy?
- Are you experiencing anger and, if so, have you verbalized it to yourself?
- Who might you be angry at?
- Can you find it in your heart to forgive them?
- Are you suppressing your anger rather than claiming it and moving on?

Take some time and reflect on the hand of God in your past. Write in a journal what you find.

CHAPTER 4

DEPRESSION

"Depression is so insidious... The fog is like a cage without a key."
~ Elisabeth Wurtzel

I believe depression has a starting point, but like with the loss of purpose—your identity—it is a shadow feeling where you cannot pinpoint the exact location of the darkness, the emptiness.

You may believe prolonged sadness is depression, and I would say we are on the same page. Sadness is a part of our lives on this side of heaven, and there is no way around that. So, when you are sad, be sad; it's okay. What's not okay is allowing it to take over your life. It's not okay having sadness become a personal attack on your character, traits, and gifts.

I had the privilege of walking two miles from the Iowa State football game, where I volunteer my time as their chaplain. On my walk, the Lord hit me with a definition of bitterness. Bitterness is a deep-rooted anger constantly fueled to anchor resentment, revenge, and hatred. If you look at bitterness as the monstrous big brother or sister of anger, you can say the same about depression. Bitterness kills its host like poison, and so does depression.

Depression is a deep-rooted sadness that reverses itself from an outward focus to inward. Like Judas, depression betrays us. It is like a slow death by a thousand cuts where one personal betrayal is not fatal. Each one is a slow bleed until you are unconscious. When you wake, you rarely remember the first time depression took a piece of you.

The scary thing is, there is no limit to sadness. But at some point, you must get up and move forward. You must stop listening to the whispers of the devil and embrace God's truths.

If you do not know or have forgotten the truth of God, grab a Bible. I grew up on King James Version but matured my faith in God's Word version. I now rock with the Christian Standard Bible and Holmes Christian Standard Bible. God's Word version helped me understand King James and I can now appreciate the classic. If you prefer, download a Bible app to get started. I like my hard copy so I can flip the pages and write in it.

Once you have your Bible, I encourage you to open up to Proverbs and read one chapter daily. I want you to read the chapter two to three times a day. There are thirty-one chapters in Proverbs, so you can do chapter one on the first day of the month and so on.

Next, I want you to read Psalms. There are 150 chapters in Psalms. Take your time reading the Psalms, preferably in a quiet place where you can reflect and master quiet time. Chew on the words—meditate on what God is saying. Feel the writer's words with delight as you think about them day and night.

From there, I recommend jumping into the Gospels of Jesus Christ, Matthew, Mark, Luke, and John. It's the same story told through four different viewpoints and written to four different audiences, with one main point. Jesus is the Messiah - Christ, the anointed, chosen son of God who came to rescue humankind from the devil and his works to have a righteous relationship with the Father for eternity.

Reading the Bible isn't a task you knock out and never read again. It's a lifelong journey. It's an ultra-marathon. Allow God to mold your heart into clay from stone. I have taken the Bible in a one year challenge. It's a monster, but I have done it many times and received many blessings because God had his hand on my heart, molding it.

Of course, you can do nothing to deserve a relationship with the heavenly father who created everything, and it's free.

Allow that to penetrate your heart.

You are worth Jesus's death and resurrection. God loves you more than you can imagine. God's love is the opposite of depression, and it's a life-giving, unspeakable, never-ending pure joy. But to get it, you must allow yourself to go on the journey with Jesus. He is omnipresent and waiting with open arms. No matter how broken you are, he will take care of you. If you are sullied, he doesn't care; he will cleanse your soul. Jesus is unconditional love.

Rewind the tape and play it back: He is omnipresent and waiting with open arms. No matter how broken you are, he will take care of you. If you are sullied, he doesn't care; he will cleanse your soul. Jesus is unconditional love.

I am not preaching at you, but work to inspire. My faith and stories come from a place of love to give hope if you are lost. I've been there.

~❖~

Playing college football for Iowa State University was a piece of the puzzle to accomplish my dream of playing in the NFL. Playing college football at an elite level solidified my identity as an athlete even more. As you know, you pay the price to pursue a worthwhile dream. You succumb to tunnel vision—one thing.

Over 99% of elite athletes identify themselves as an athlete to the core. We were nothing else, thought of nothing else, did nothing else. They did not train us on how to separate our personal identity from our athletic profession. The training of a high performance athlete is always shortsighted. As a result, once the game is done with us, we lose our identity.

When I arrived on the Iowa State gridiron, I realized quickly that we had a very good running back that was honored in and around Iowa. His hometown was Nebraska, so he wasn't too far from family. He was a bruiser of defenses and built like a brick house. He aspired to play in the NFL, as do 99% of people on the team and around the nation. After his senior year, he entered the NFL draft. Unbeknownst to him, his last time stepping on the field in the Iowa State uniform would be his last time playing the game he loved.

We never knew how many stages of athletic transition he went through, but I can tell you the results of getting stuck in one. Depression eats at your soul and steps on your character. You are instigated by dark thoughts of being worthless. The rejection and dark self-talk of depression is internally deafening and externally silent while it makes its thousand cuts. He eventually lost his battle and took his life. It was only two short years after playing for Iowa State—they found my teammate dead under a bridge.

I was told that one hour before his death, his grandparents called 911, stating he was threatening suicide. The police made a house call and interviewed him, concluding he would not harm himself and he was not under the influence of any substance. They left. About an hour later, he walked out of the house in twenty-six-degree weather without a jacket and didn't return. The police dispatch received numerous calls reporting a young black man jumped off a bridge to his death.

The voice of depression told him he was worthless because he did not accomplish his ultimate dream. The truth is he loved football, but football stopped loving him once college was over. He was lost, with no vision of how to come back. He had been forgotten—written off.

Before he left his house that day, he left a final message. He turned all the posters of himself around to face the wall. His aspirations of the NFL were over, so he determined his life was too. The sad thing is, I know if he were alive today, my teammate and friend would be an inspiring and legendary thirty-nine-year-old husband, father, and maybe a thriving superstar in his own right and his community.

Unfortunately, my friend is not the only victim of depression. There was another guy I had the privilege of battling against on the gridiron every year. I only knew him from afar as a competitor, but he was a heck of a player and one of the few white defensive backs on the field. So, you know he had to be a dawg out there. He was athletic and a big hitter. Offensive players always knew where he was because he struck fear into their hearts.

In college, they named him a two-time all-conference player in one of the top five conferences in Division One FBS play. So, you know he was an elite football player. He was awarded a shot at his dream of playing in the NFL by being drafted in the sixth round. He was there for two seasons. While in the NFL, he collected a few stats and earned a Super Bowl championship.

Going into his third season, they cut him from the team that drafted him. No other team picked him up, so he began his athletic transition. In his native state, he was a god. People loved him, but I had the opportunity of running into him roughly two years after his stint in the NFL. He remembered who I was, and we traded pleasantries, but something about him stuck out to me. He seemed happy on the outside, but his eyes said otherwise.

What's that saying? "The eyes are the windows to the soul," by William Shakespeare.

I wish I had run into him two years later because when I first saw him, I wasn't in the ministry yet and wasn't equipped to spot hidden pain. His smile was bright, but his eyes were black deep, bottomless pits of sorrow. He needed someone to show him his value as a person—not financial value. On the surface, he was doing fine as a speaker and entrepreneur.

The following year, after running into him, I heard he had overdosed on a mixture of drugs. Intentionally or unintentionally, he was battling an identity crisis and had unresolved pain.

As athletes, we are never taught, or we forget that the sport is an avenue to reach your true greatness—your calling. The sport or being an athlete is only a piece of you.

Think about the abundant wealth of God. He created the heavens and the earth. God created you to do great things. In this life, the sport is only an avenue to allow you to be what he made you to be. He wants you to be great for his glory. Football was not my friend's greatness; it was a vehicle for him to reach his calling. My colleague was fine financially, but was a lost soul.

Now you are on a journey to find the call to maximize the greatness God placed in you. When you understand that there is life after the sport, you can move forward and push past the depression.

You are more than your gifts and talents as an athlete. Remember, it is all fleeting.

Peter 1:24-25: "for all flesh is like grass, in all its glory like the flower of the grass. The grass withers and the flowers fall, but the word of the Lord endures forever. And this is the word that was preached as the gospel to you." Holman's Christian Standard Bible.

You are valuable and worthy. God loves you—yes, you! He sacrificed himself and his son for you. Why? So that you can have an eternal relationship with the creator of heaven and earth. You only have to surrender, trusting in Jesus as your Lord and savior. Sign that letter of commitment and step into your new life led by the ultimate leader, Jesus Christ.

I am a recipient of the transformational power of God, the father, Jesus the son, and the Holy Spirit. What I know is when you surrender, what they can give is greater than anything you or anyone else has for you. It is not complicated. While there is no sinner prayer or any prayer that will automatically make you a Christian. God is a God of the heart. To be a Christian is about your heart's posture toward them and your commitment you give in your heart. Being Christian is simply: Trust plus belief equals faith. Trust in who God is, plus believing in the promises of God equals faith in God. Trust, belief, and faith lead to truth and greatness.

COACHING SESSION

Read Psalm 1:1-3

- What does this verse say to you?
- I want you to imagine being the tree and what your life will look like after doing verses 1 and 2.
- If you are sad, have you named it and shared your sadness with another person or God?
- Go get a journal and take some time to write about how you feel about transitioning.

Read Jeremiah 29:11-14a

- Verse 11: How does it make you feel that God has a plan for you and your life?
- Verse 12: How does it make you feel to know that God hears and is listening to you?
- Verse 13-14: How does it make you feel to know God will allow you to find him?
- Have you allowed yourself to feel sad instead of fighting it?

CHAPTER 5

GLORY CHASING

"If any man seeks for greatness, let him forget greatness and ask for truth, and he will find both."
~ Horace Mann

Your entire life revolved around chasing the glory—your greatness. The path was clear: playing sports, going to school, and balancing a social life. Being a high-performance athlete takes work and intentionality. The entire time you believed the perfect grades, the high-ranking stats were your greatness. The mistake in this belief is the sport—the athlete in you—is not your truth.

So, when you believe God created you for greatness, but then it has stopped in one of the most important areas of your life, then what? You are no longer using your gifts in the world of sports for whatever reason. The reason could be you got injured or cut, your team sucked, or no one called you. But for whatever reason, the pursuit of your dream has stopped.

You are now asking, what am I going to do? Who am I? What am I good at? The crazy thing is that this doesn't hit you like a ton of bricks. No, this lingers in your mind since the pursuit of your dream is officially over.

In my athletic transition, I went through anger, avoidance, and depression. I had those questions, and I'm pretty sure you have them, too. Let me tell you, there is nothing wrong with asking these types of questions. These are critical questions for you to dive deeper into as they give you clarity on your new journey. In fact, it's great you are asking these questions because it means you are now moving forward and thinking about the future.

They saying curiosity killed the cat, so it's a good thing you're a dawg because you're hunting for the bone to own.

Now, this part of the transition will hurt because you are chasing after your greatness. It is close and you know it. You know what it smells like—what it feels like—but you cannot see it or touch it because it is a different game. Now, you are trying to find that thing you can dedicate blood, sweat, and tears to. You have to find the glory beyond the sport. Often, we speak of fortune,—yes, money—but deep in your core, you know that money is not the answer. It's just a quick fix. Chasing your glory is all about chasing your greatness, and once you catch it, you and the world will know what it is. Until then, you are on the hunt. I would go as far as to say you are hunting for your life.

If you are like me, you are an idea machine. The unsolicited advice will come from everywhere. There will be yes-men who will love every idea you come up with. You will have those that don't get it and tell you to get a real job. Some of these people will be haters, and some will be oblivious cheerleaders for any concept. It is essential to keep moving forward and see everything for what it is because your greatness waits for you to find it.

Like many athletes, I had an excellent plan for my life. I was going to be an NFL player collecting my money and then creating a gummy factory. Yep, I was going to be the black Willy Wonka developing gummies in the shape of football players in different colors based on NFL teams. On the wrapper, you would see the players you were eating, depending on the color of the gummy. Yes, I know this is a million-dollar, maybe a billion-dollar idea. If you do it, I ask you to shoot me back a 5% royalty check off each bag.

What did Ace Hood say, "baby needs shoes..."

I will share my glory chasing ideas with you, and you better not laugh. No, I'm just playing—laugh away because I pray someday you will laugh at yours. Here it goes:

- Creating a dessert restaurant
- NASCAR driver
- stunt double
- creating a grilled cheese restaurant
- creating a hot dog restaurant

- building apparel and brand merch
- legal document interpreter
- sports recruiting software developer
- ultimate handyman
- laundry mat owner
- real estate investor
- stock market investor
- create next helmet to prevent head injuries
- pen manufacturer
- YouTuber
- Podcaster
- motivational speaker
- professional football coach
- Olympian hurdler
- jewelry salesman
- author
- personal trainer
- teacher
- firefighter
- commercial actor
- board game developer

I pursued some of these, others were ideas never released until now. Some of these ideas I shared with people, and then they dissipated into clouds of ideas. I had zero qualifications like a NASCAR driver, a software developer, or a manufacturer of pens. But just because I didn't have the background doesn't mean I should not pursue them. Of course, some of these ideas needed to stay an idea and not be pursued, but if I had not explored these ideas, some things I did would not have happened.

Okay, now that you stopped laughing—some of these ideas I pursued, and some took up residence in my mind for a hot second. Some I prayed over, and they ran away. Others fired me up until I realized the work behind them. One of my favorite ideas that I am still proud of is the last one. I took the game of rock-paper-scissors and turned it into a dice game. That idea went from conception to reality, giving me a sense of accomplishment. After finding a manufacturer, I had my prototype and called Hasbro. They gave me a rejection letter saying, "we do not take outside games." The game sits where I can see it every day and smile. I have played it with my kids many times, and they loved it.

I share this with you because I want you to realize that even though your athletic career is over and you are transitioning into a new greatness; you have terrific things inside of you, and it's up to you to allow them to come into existence. God uniquely designed each one of us for greatness in our own right. Look at yourself in the mirror and say I have been created to do great things.

Embrace the glory chase and understand that this is part of your transition. You are looking for your greatness because it is playing hide and seek. There are multiple places to look, but I have discovered that it likes to hide in the past of forgotten visions, passions, or loves.

Explore, explore, and explore some more is my encouragement to you. But I warn you; this isn't a skip through the meadows of roses and rainbows. It's more like the garden of poisoned thorns and gloomy skies because you will throw all you got into these ideas, and as you run with passion, you realize this one is not it. You will share your ideas with friends and have great enthusiasm, but then you hit exhaustion and defeat.

They say the definition of insanity is doing something repeatedly, expecting a different result. But in this case, you will do the same thing over and over again and get a different result. The result you are looking for is your greatness; the only way you will find it is through trial and error. It is like the 10,000 times Benjamin Franklin tried to invent the incandescent light bulb; He never failed. He just found 10,000 ways that didn't work.

It will take patience and it may cause you to slide back into depression because you feel worthless. You feel you have failed. Fight against the thoughts, get up, and keep pushing. This is part of the process; the more you tell yourself this, the better off you will be. You are valued and have a ton to offer, but the world isn't ready for it yet, or you have not developed far enough. Failure is an opportunity to learn something new.

In the next stage, you will see that God revealed my calling in pursuit of my greatness and he will do the same for you as you journey through glory chasing.

Remember, as you chase glory, don't forget that you must make ends meet. Don't shortchange yourself and fail to build a life because you have not found your greatness. The princess had to kiss a few frogs before she found her Prince. You will have to do a few jobs that suck to find out what you want to do.

In stage five, we will see a few guys in their callings, but I warn you, and please don't forget this: sometimes your greatness isn't found in your career. If you put your greatness into your career, you are setting yourself up for another identity crisis.

As I was going through my journey of chasing glory, my calling was being developed through all the trials and tribulations, the misfires, and frustrations.

My first job out of college was being a bouncer at a bar, and I was the absolute worst bouncer, because I allowed anyone brave enough to give me an ID into the bar and the last one to every fight. Observation taught me that those who break up fights also get hit in the face—I was too good-looking for that! I also drank all the strawberry soda.

My next job was being an assistant manager at Helzberg Diamonds. I was selling diamonds, but the pay was meager; my fiancée (college girlfriend) told me I needed a better job. Every time I remind her of our conversations back then, she doesn't remember saying that because she's like, "wow, that's really rude." Nevertheless, it needed to happen. It needed to be said. So, I took a job as a phone team representative taking eighty-plus calls daily, most of which were unpleasant. Because the money was good, I liked the hours and built a life.

I began to build a career, but there was still the loss of greatness, and I had to find it. To start, I became a football and track coach for a local high school, coaching my two favorite sports. I loved helping the athletes develop and achieve their desires. It wasn't my calling, but I got my fix of greatness through coaching again.

During those four years, my joy at work dwindled, even though I excelled at my job and won awards. In my corporate job, the pay allowed me to buy a house, build my credit, and get married. We began to build our family and build a life. My life looked really good with a corporate job, coaching high school sports, and building a life. Everything was going well on the outside, but I knew deep in my soul I was called to do more impactful work; but what? So, the hunt truly began.

My point is, while chasing your glory, build a life, and earn money for the future. Dream about the life you want in your home. I'm not talking about money, vacations, cars, and stuff; I'm talking about your deep heart's desires. Consider the climate and culture of your home—the joy of your marriage, having babies!

But first, get a pet and enjoy your marriage before adding little humans to the mix. Enjoy the pleasure of your friendships. Build up your savings, buy some assets, and learn a craft, but don't forget to find a healthy, Jesus-loving, Bible-believing church. That is your number one priority. Build a life over a career. Finally, play games, and enjoy the gifts of God. Every magnificent gift comes from Him.

In the end, after all my glory chasing, my calling was not to be found. It poked its head out when I volunteered to coach at a local high school. It was deep within my soul, yet I still couldn't recognize what it looked like. I knew I was on the right track, but I was walking in the dark. Of course, this wasn't the end of my story, and it will not be yours. You should believe that if you fail to find your calling, keep the faith—it is part of the process.

Like the good book says, you have to walk by faith, not by sight. There is no faith if you can see what's on the other side. You live under God's understanding and not your own.

COACHING SESSION

Take your journal and answer these questions:

- When you reflect on your future life, what do you desire in your heart? (Not money and stuff)

- What have you learned from falling, not failing?

- What are you chasing?

- Are you creating a life while you chase your glory?

- Where are you investing your time as a free leader (volunteer)?

CHAPTER 6

CALLING

"Trust in the Lord with all your heart and lean not on your own understanding; in all your ways acknowledge Him, And He shall direct your paths."
~ Proverbs 3:5-6

Have you ever heard of a story of the prodigal son? If not, there was this farmer who had two sons. If this were a Disney movie, the athletes would be very handsome with every attribute known to man. Wait for it; it sounds like reality a little. Being an elite, well-trained athlete like yourself, you fit the mold.

This farmer had a bag, and his sons knew they would inherit his fortune. So, one day, the youngest son steps to his father and says, "Yo, pops, I'm done with this farming stuff. I'm trying to make a name for myself and see what I can gain on my journey. I'm gonna need my bag now—you know, my inheritance—while you are still alive."

The farmer gives his youngest son his inheritance on the spot. Being a father for some time now, I can assume he knew this day would come with his youngest boy, that free spirit and all. So, the son sets off to the big city and goes ham. He's out there wasting his money sleeping with prostitutes and trying out the latest treats (drugs) for spiritual connectedness, enlightenment and what not.

I could see him wasting his money by buying out the bar. Someone who gets their money fast usually spends it faster than they gained it, so you know he rocked the latest gear from shoes, pants, shirts, and hats to jewelry. But one day, a famine hit. You can call that a recession, depression, war, crash, or even pandemic. To put it all together, everything stopped, and people ran out of money, including him.

Bouncing around from employer to employer looking for work, they all said no. All his so-called friends disappeared. Unlike the prodigal son, I still had my friends, but when football was over for me, I was introduced to real living amid the Great Recession. The son found a job with a hog farmer, and I found a job as a bouncer. The son came from wealth. I too came from wealth in a way because I had a college degree paid for by the football team. Don't get it twisted; I grew up missing many things money could buy, if you know what I mean. My mom did her best and is my hero, but we still lacked a few things.

One day, this young man came to his senses. He was so malnourished and hurting; he ate pig slop. I am not sure what pig slop tastes like, but I bet you have to be down bad to eat with the pigs. You would need to be in an unhealthy situation for a long time to think pig slop is the way to go. His boss thought so too.

Luckily, this young man had some wits about him and realized his father's workers were eating better than him. The prodigal son returned home and begged for a job under his father.

Every day, the farmer looked out toward the long driveway, hoping to see his son in the distance. That day finally came. The father got up, ran to his son, and embraced him with more love than he could have imagined. The son begins to beg and plead for forgiveness because he sinned toward God, our heavenly father, and his earthly father. The farmer was so excited to have his son back he anoints him with the family robe. He tells his employees to cook up a feast. "Fire the grill! We're having a block party because my son has returned."

I tell you this biblical story because I was the son. You are the son; the rest will come when we surrender our chase to The Father. It's difficult to do this; it takes humility. That's why I'm going to tell you the story of my darkest moment, the basement, rock-bottom experience. But before I tell you mine, I want to share a few short teammate stories to about getting stuck in anger and glory chasing.

First, I have many teammates stuck in one of the four first stages of athletic transition. One stuck in glory chasing found himself in a high-speed chase running from the cops on a dirt bike. Little did he know this would be his last major feat as he hit a guardrail and died instantly. This is the shortest story.

In reality, most athletes are done competing in their twenties. Only a few make it to the professional level. The number is roughly 1% when you isolate the particular sport. Once someone makes it to the league, they only last about five years, given the sport. In football, the average NFL career is around three years. That's a lot of work for little dream. My NFL dream began at five. Most young men develop their dream between the ages of five and ten. Athletes don't see their dream come to fruition until they hit around the age of twenty-two. The dream is relatively simple, and that is to be an NFLer.

Both my teammate and I missed out on the NFL dream for various reasons. As I progressed through the six stages of athletic transition, my teammate found himself stuck in the anger stage. This stagnant positioning placed him in environments to release his bitterness and frustration on all who popped open the can. Sometimes he would leave victorious from a brawl, but this last time, his anger got the best of him. Thinking he was fighting one, not realizing there were two opponents, the other came up behind him and hit him in the head with a life-ending blow. For weeks he was in the hospital fighting for his life, and he lost the battle.

Then there is being stuck in glory chasing.

Bang! Bang! Multiple times, this was the last sound he heard.

I had a teammate who was a year older than me, who had greatness written all over him. He set multiple records as a true freshman in a top division for college football. God blessed him with unbelievable talent. His dreams of the NFL were paved with gold from heaven. Throughout his career, from college to the professionals, he would make decisions that put him in hot water. His talents began dissipating as they do for everyone, and he was eventually cut. He continued pursuing his dream because he didn't want to let it go, but his talents were dwindling. After pursuing it for quite some time, he hung up the cleats. He chose a career that brought fast cash, but with fast cash comes a few consequences. My teammate became a drug dealer back in his hometown.

I can assume he was great at his job, as he was with most things when he put his mind to it. I can safely assume again some people didn't admire his skills. On this day, he was alone at his grandmother's house, and some of his competitors knew of this. With no regard for who was in the house, they pulled up and fired bullets through the walls, doors, and windows, killing my teammate on the spot.

~❖~

Reflecting on the lives of all my teammates who were and are stuck in athletic transition, I wonder what their lives would be like. I know they would have accomplished amazing feats. They would have shattered records and sailed to new heights because I see it over and over with the teammates who have transitioned well.

I have interviewed over 500 former athletes in various sports and some females. I've only found three former athletes who did not go through the six stages of athletic transition. That means 99% of athletes will experience some form of athletic transition; don't be like the ones who get stuck. I have said this many times throughout the book; the answer is giving up your life to Jesus Christ as your Lord and savior. He will take you farther than you could ever imagine when you let him lead. You will experience life beyond your dreams. I never made it to the NFL, but I can tell you the life I have—I wouldn't trade it for anything. I would not go back in time and go to the NFL if I had the chance because I would lose everything I have now.

The secret is to identify where you are. You know the four negative stages of athletic transition and you must speak them into existence. Cast those negative demons out of your way and out of your life. There is so much life in front of you waiting to be captured. God has specifically designated work for you to do, and you are called to find it and totally dominate it. God has something for you, but you are the only one who can open that gift. You are the only one that will be led to your gift. The world needs you to allow Jesus to lead your life so we can reap the benefits from the blessings of your greatness that God has designed specifically for you.

I know because I faced the same journey and found truth. I found my greatness and calling.

Looking up at the stars peering into the heavens, I cried my soul out. I faced the hardest thing I had ever dealt with. I was about to lose my family. My oldest son was almost welcomed into the cycle of another broken home under the Sumrall lineage. Recalling how long it took me to win my wife's heart back, I can tell you that if it wasn't by God's grace, there wouldn't be a Team Sumrall with four beautiful children.

In my glory chasing and consumption of alcohol, I pursued another woman and was on the verge of cheating on my wife. Forgetting about it and not thinking much of it, my older brother-in-law gave me an ultimatum the following week. "You tell my sister, or I will."

Walking through the Athletic Transition is not for the weak. Only warriors can continue to walk through hell, and you are a warrior! But you have to yield humility as one of your weapons.

My wife and I work together; our cubicles are only a few bodies away. One day, pulling her aside, I told her about my bad choices. I'm so grateful I didn't do the deed, but it wasn't because I decided not to; intoxicated and stupid, I was totally on board. God allowed me to go so far into my desires so that I could see where I was leading myself.

Why did he set it up to block me? Why is it God did not allow me to follow my stupidity further? Why was the situation only set up for word exchange and nothing more?

I have no clue why God was so gracious, but I am forever thankful for his protection.

After sharing with my wife what I had done, I felt sick to my stomach. So sick I went to my boss and asked to leave because I wasn't feeling well. I got in my car, went straight to the church, and sat in the top row. Praying and pleading, I asked God to please give her the strength to forgive me. Give her the strength not to leave me. I wanted to be a great husband—I wanted to be a great father. God knew my heart's desires, and he knows yours as well.

I don't remember all the details because my brain blanked out some things. What I do remember is I had to lead a high school football team as their head coach; wow, behind the scenes, I ruined my family. Leading my team into a football game, I can tell you I was the worst coach in history. My body was there, but everything else was in deep shame, guilt, and sorrow. After the game, I apologized to my brother-in-law for my drunken stupidity. I went home, and you can imagine the climate in my house. I assumed it was terrible but don't remember all the details. At the time, my oldest child was two months old, and like me, he would live without his biological father in his home.

Later that night, I stepped out of the house and sat on a retaining wall, peering through the stars and praying to God. The most significant thing in my life happened at that moment because I stepped off the throne of my life and gave up the seat to Jesus Christ, not just to be my savior, but to be my lord and king.

As I sobbed, with eyes to heaven, I said something that transformed my life and opened the doors to the path where my greatness hid. "Lord, I can't be king of my life anymore. I am stepping off the throne. Please be the king of my life and direct me. I will go wherever you direct me."

Jesus became more than my savior for eternal damnation that instant. That moment was the burning Bush moment for me. It was the opening of the Red Sea. It was the empty tomb of Jesus Christ. That single point in time was the beginning of who I am today.

My life did not just become easy after I stepped off the throne and Jesus took over. I still had a battle to fight, a new journey to quest, and a beauty to rescue. *Wild at Heart* by John Eldredge comes to mind. God came through and redeemed my young marriage. As of this writing, we have been married for twelve years and have at least fifty more to go. We have four amazing children aged ten, six and six, and a three-year-old. Three boys, and the youngest is our little princess. Look at what God can do when you give it all to him.

My wife is the beauty I rescued, and boy is she. I'll tell you the battles never end, but God is good. Even though Jesus became king and my marriage was redeemed, I still hunted for my calling and my greatness. Oh, how the journey is sweet because it's never about the destination, no matter how much we want to get there.

Between the time I knew my dream would not come true, to the moment I hit rock bottom, I hated my life because I did not achieve my dream. I worked in corporate for four years, which I hated, but I loved coaching football and track for those four years. Every day I went to work, and it sucked the life out of me. Yes, I accomplished a lot at my job, but it wasn't what I was made to do by the design of our Father in heaven, and I knew that to my core. Hiding deep within my soul, I knew I was supposed to coach people. So, I looked at my gift sets and concluded that I could train people to accomplish their heart's desires.

I created a company called LYFE Changing Fitness. LYFE was an acronym meaning Live Your Future Every day. The plan was to train athletes in speed, agility, and strength to help them become more well-rounded athletes. I received a few desirable clients, but most were homemakers and stay-at-home moms. My niche was bringing the gym to them and help them with their nutrition. My traveling training company was moving in the right direction but wasn't getting the desired clients. The focus was to train athletes, not stay-at-home moms and wives. I didn't have a facility, so living in the Midwest from late fall to early spring had some outdoor complications.

With numerous prayers, I continued asking God to lead my life, to lead my company and to make it something that glorifies him. God heard my prayers, took over my company, and shut the doors. All that money and time, and all the education was gone, but it was gone for what was to come.

After the closing of LYFE, I went back on the hunt for my greatness. I was still working in corporate and coaching high school sports. While doing that, I had this strange desire to create a Bible study, but I wasn't confident in stepping into that leadership role. I started cracking my Bible open with a new focus because I knew I would find my calling in God's word. I would read book after book in the Bible.

This went on for two years and in that time, I still hated my job, but I didn't hate my life because Jesus was in control. Suddenly, I found my greatness, and it was to love people and bring them to the feet of Jesus.

Now, this is crazy. During my four years in corporate, I became friends with an atheist who loved trying to tell me why God doesn't exist. This made me go harder because I'm not a debater and need to understand my faith. Next, I became friends with a guy who grew up in a very strict Christian denomination and family. He went to seminary to become a pastor, but eventually quit. Now he is all about evolution and the big bang theory. Again, this made me go harder into the word of God and see how science is under God's authority. I had another coworker friend who came out as gay, and we had an excellent Q&A session about Jesus and being gay. This made me look deeper into God's design of humans.

God made me go deeper into a relationship with him, but not necessarily to debate with my friends. Then I was reminded of the encounter with my pastor when I was twelve. If you recall from earlier in the book, my pastor told me he had a vision from God that I would be a pastor.

At the time of that vision, I was not a Christian, nor did I want to be a Christian because I judged the king by his citizens. There was also the small detail of the arrest for shoplifting two days prior, unbeknownst to my pastor. I rejected that vision but chose the idea of being a Christian motivational speaker. I still do not see myself leading a church as I write this.

My version of the pastor's vision led me to study motivational speakers like Les Brown and Jim Rohn. In my search for various motivational speakers, I found Eric Thomas, the hip-hop preacher. I fell in love with his message.

~❖~

God puts people in your life to draw you nearer to him. One day I was walking my oldest in his stroller, and one of my athletes rode his bike by me. He said, "Coach, you were a part of FCA (Fellowship of Christian Athletes)?"

I was wearing my FCA shirt from college. He asked me if I would like to speak at the high school FCA. I felt like this was my moment—I was ready to begin my speaking career. I was presented with my opportunity to become a great Christian motivational speaker, and I knew this was of God.

We set it up for me to speak in October, which is a very special month for me. If you remember, I was told I would be a pastor in October—I gave my life to Jesus as my savior in October. October is when I hit my rock bottom, giving Jesus the throne of my life. So, I knew I was about to step into my calling and greatness. When October came, I received a phone call stating they had to move my opportunity to speak at their FCA huddle because they double booked. They moved me to December nineteenth, which gave me even more time to prepare this killer message.

The day came, and I was hyped. It was like going into my first college football game, where the nerves were crazy. This was my first speaking engagement, but I was confident in my skills. I had props and my wife filming my message. The message was locked and loaded. I was ready to shake and shock the world.

That was the worst presentation I have ever done in my entire life.

I was reflecting with my wife recently about the first speaking opportunity, and she recalls me saying to her, "No one will ever see this video!" The message was great. I still remember it, even though it was many years ago. It was the deliverance that was terrible. It was me who was awful. I forgot pieces of the message while I was speaking. My mind went blank numerous times. I stuttered, shaking uncontrollably in front of all the high school students. Even though the deliverance was trash, but God used it.

Three weeks later, I received a random phone call from an unknown number. I'm in the middle of work taking calls and such, but something inside me said to pick it up. I answered the phone, and it was the state director of the FCA of Iowa. He asked me if I was interested in a full-time job with the FCA.

God used my terrible presentation in only a way that he could use it. The FCA staffer was at the event, heard me speak, and thought I did a great job. He thought I did such a great job that he passed my name to the state director.

When the director asked me about employment with the FCA, all I could think about was the FCA person for my football team at Iowa State. His relationship with me was one of the main reasons I gave my life to Jesus as my savior. I thought if I could be like him, I'm all in. It only took me about two seconds to respond to the state director, and I said let's meet in two hours. We met at a Panera Bread, and nine months later, I began my ministry journey.

When I was twelve, two days after being arrested for shoplifting, my pastor told me I would be a pastor. Sixteen years later, I stepped into a pastoral role, but not for the church, but for my Heavenly Father. My greatness is to bring people to the feet of Jesus. I initially thought I would find my greatness through my calling through the things I did while I was glory chasing. But that was not where it was hiding. It was hiding in my past, and it was hiding in God's word. It was hiding in my passion for helping athletes. It was hiding in my journey.

My calling is not my greatness, and my identity is not wrapped up in being a pastor. My identity is wrapped up in being a child of God. My calling is God's vehicle to release the greatness he has designed me for.

I love working for the Lord and pray God will bless me with the ability to have a long life and work for him until I see him for eternity. However, that is my greatness, and you need to understand that just because it is my greatness to work for the Lord, that doesn't mean that is your greatness.

God will put people in your path, set your boundaries, and allow situations to happen—good or bad—so that you to seek and find him. That's why you have this book in your hand. God wants you so much that he gave me the strength, protection, energy, and wisdom to put all this together for your calling through him, who is forever. I pray over you, and you are loved.

Yes, put your trust, hopes, dreams, fears, concerns, and life in Jesus's kingship. Give your identity to the Lord. When you say I am..., you are locking your identity in the thing that comes after *I am*. I am a Christian—I am a child of God. Plug your heart into your I am. Commit your daily walk into that I am, which you are.

Trust plus belief equals faith. It's a daily journey until our Father calls us home. But remember this: God is a God of the heart, and your heart is where your life flows from. The first four stages are all about your heart. You must guard your heart.

> "From one man, throughout the whole earth. He decided beforehand when they should fall and turned their bodies. His purpose was for the nation to seek after him and perhaps feel their way toward him and find him" Acts 17:26-27 New Living Translation.

God has a wonderful plan for you. Have faith in Him and put one foot in front of the other. Trust He will make a way out of no way and watch him do it. You were created to do wonderful things. Finding your greatness—it's just like dating.

When you are striving to find that person you want to have a relationship with, it seems like they run away from you, and it's extremely hard, but when you stop and focus on developing and loving yourself, that's when they come. When you focus on God and His plan, things start to fall into place. Stop striving under your own power; begin thriving under God's power and watch Him work.

Here are a few examples of the greatness released from others and their calling based on our extensive interviews with others:

- Greatness: Help kids get to college / Calling: Entrepreneur and Volunteer Football Coach

- Greatness: Serve the underprivileged youth / Calling: Community Center Director
- Greatness: Show athletes they can be great cops / Calling: Police Officer
- Greatness: Show athletes they can be great firefighter / Calling: Firefighter
- Greatness: Authentic leader / Calling: Actor, Director, Producer
- Greatness: Gospel philanthropist / Calling: Entrepreneur
- Greatness: Developing young men / Calling: College Coaching

Our greatness is our why. It's our driving force, and a calling is the means that allows us to maximize our greatness. Your job doesn't always connect to your greatness, but it allows you to do it. When I was coaching sports, I worked in the corporate world. My cousin is an entrepreneur, which allows him to coach football and run his nonprofit that takes kids around the country to visit colleges and play flag football tournaments to showcase their talents.

The Lord knows what's best for you. Trust in Him, build a life, develop yourself in all facets, and learn to love yourself as Jesus loves you. Build relationships and keep moving forward. It's impossible to build a greatness, and it's hard to find it, so let God do the dirty work, and in due time it will reveal itself, and when it does, don't let fear hold you back.

Now, all of this comes with a warning: when your greatness reveals itself, there will be an unknown future awaiting you. There will be uncertainty.

Rewind the tape and play it back: when your greatness reveals itself, there will be an unknown future awaiting you. There will be uncertainty.

There will be challenges, but that is the path you must take. The trail is narrow and unpaved, filled with potholes and ruts, but just like the path with Jesus, so is the path to one's calling, which would reveal their greatness. Take this to the bank not because I said it, but because God said it. Faith and fear cannot coexist within you.

"Be strong and courageous. Do not be afraid or discouraged. For the Lord, your God, is with you wherever you go." Joshua 1:9 New Living Translation.

Here is something that can help you understand the essence of fear and the essence of faith:

F.E.A.R. is the Lack of Belief + Lack of Trust

F.E.A.R is False – Evidence – Appearing – Real

F.A.I.T.H. is Belief + Trust

F.A.I.T.H is Fully – Anticipating – It – To – Happen

Step into it, trust the Lord and watch Him work.

COACHING SESSION

- What is keeping you from letting God lead your steps?

- What are you so passionate about that you would do it for free?

- Do you have an opportunity in front of you that has much uncertainty, but it's something you cannot not do?

- Is there something you are running from? What is it and why?

Take some time and ask God to reveal your pre-assigned greatness.

CHAPTER 7

APPRECIATION

"Appreciation is the highest form of prayer, for it acknowledges the presence of good wherever you shine the light of your thankful thoughts."
~ Alan Cohen

Appreciation is a sweet-tasting fruit. It has nothing and everything to do with you. It took me ten years to reach this stage.

Appreciation is like when a grandparent sits back and watches their child play with their grandchild in pure bliss. Appreciation is stopping to enjoy the fruits of your labor. Appreciation has unspeakable joy oozing out of it.

You want to get to appreciation, but you cannot bypass the first four stages of transition. They need to be so far removed that they no longer speak up and startle you. You cannot reach appreciation until you have indifference toward the first four stages. They will pop up, but you show them no satisfaction. They may come back with vengeance, but every time they rear their ugly head, putting you back into anger, avoidance, depression, and glory chasing, unflinching, you move forward.

When I was a kid, I had this hallway between the living room in our bedrooms and the restroom ducked off to the side with a mini hallway. There were no windows, so it was always dark. One of my missions was to startle my stepdad. Anytime the opportunity presented itself, I went into hiding, chomping at the bit to get him. He would walk by and I would take advantage of the moment and jump out, trying to scare him; every time I was defeated. I have never startled my stepdad. My stepdad never flinched; he was in control when I jumped. This is the same way you have to handle the first four stages when they jump out and try to startle you. This is when you are ready for appreciation.

In my ten-year journey, from the NFL combine, college pro days, and the NFL draft, there was a trace of anger, depression, chasing, and questioning. I would see guys who played my position with stats equal or less, getting their shot at accomplishing their childhood dream. Guys whose combined or Pro Day numbers being overshadowed by what I produced at my Pro Day when I was pursuing the NFL and they at least got a tryout. I would be happy for them but also sad for myself. This would go on for days. I felt I should have received a fair shot, but life isn't fair.

It was after my thirtieth birthday that appreciation began to develop. I remember watching the NFL draft and envisioned myself being on an NFL team. As I saw the selection of players scroll through, I thought these guys would be my replacement. I realized that being thirty in the professional world of sports, they considered you a dinosaur. Thinking about my body and how much pain I was in, I realized my body would want and scream for me to stop. This was when I realized that the dream of being in the NFL is long gone forever, and that was okay.

For the next two years, I realized my NFL dreams as a player would be over. I was pretty confident I would be ready to move on and create a new career. At thirty-two to thirty-three, appreciation was breaking ground and becoming a tall tree.

One athlete I coached in high school who played my position and wore my number in high school and college is now making a name for himself in the NFL. I was still so blessed that God allowed me to be a part of his development in his professional dream.

This gratitude and enjoyment continued to grow as I saw guys I ministered get their shot at their NFL dreams. I talked about guys I played against in college and high school out of joy rather than rivalry and negativity.

That was the first half of the appreciation stage. The second half was being able to reflect on my entire sports journey with a smile rather than seeing myself as a failure.

God is good—a protector and provider—but we have to trust him. We must believe that he has a plan for us that's greater than anything we could ever imagine or dream. I truly believe if God had not protected me from the NFL, sure I would have made some serious money, but my beautiful wife would not be with me. I would have fallen prey to the promiscuous woman or women. Illegitimate children or an STD were in my future. No, this is not saying others are like this, but my character, morals, values, and commitment were not Jesus-led. You read my story and know these things are true for me. My tree of knowledge of good and evil is greed, ambition, and sexual sin. I believe God was protecting me from me.

Going into the NFL would have ruined me or maybe even killed me, and I would not have my wonderful babies. I would not be chasing after this—my lord and savior. I would not have found my greatness of bringing people to the feet of Jesus.

Now, the privilege of witnessing many athletes give their lives to Jesus is mine. I have had the opportunity of baptizing men and even my oldest son. The Lord God has allowed me to live in my unique preordained greatness, and he has one for you as well that will unleash you for his glory.

He loves you so much that he allowed his only son to die for you. Now, as a father of four, I couldn't do that for anyone, even if I had the power to bring them back to life. If God loves you that much and has already demonstrated that with Jesus's flogging, sacrifice, and death on the cross, don't you think he has a wonderful plan for your life?

I love you, and that is why I wrote this book.

1,000,000 IS THE GOAL

Message from the Author,

Athletes no matter if they are current, transitioning, or former are very important to me and that is why I write. Please stay connected to Sumrall Coaching by going to www. sumrallcoaching.com and exhaust all the resources that have been developed for you as you embark on this new journey. For further learning and encouragement, I suggest reading other books I have created for your benefit.

Finally, I have one personal favor to ask. Books written by R.J. Sumrall under Sumrall Coaching are self-published. As such there are no publishing house backing it with money and pushing it on the public. To offset this disadvantage, I ask you to leave and online review with your endorsement.

Better still, if this book helped you, I ask you to refer this book to a teammate, family member, friend, or competitor who is seeking solutions to identify their greatness.

Take a moment and purchase a copy as a gift or send a picture recommending, they get one for themselves. Without referrals this book will remain obscure. I have an audacious goal of helping 1,000,000 athletes transition well and find their greatness. The only way this goal will be met is by your help in getting the word out.

Visit www.sumrallcoaching.com for other book on maximizing your greatness.

Speaker Request: rj@sumrallcoaching.com

Sumrall Coaching Workshop: rj@sumrallcoaching.com

Personal Coaching Sessions: rj@sumrallcoaching.com

Keep Being Awesome for Jesus!

R.J. Sumrall

NOTES

NOTES

NOTES

NOTES

NOTES

NOTES

NOTES

Made in the USA
Monee, IL
14 May 2025